Right From The Beginning

EILEEN DISTASIO-CLARK

Copyright © 2024

All Rights Reserved

With Great Love and Appreciation to Those Who Have and Do Bless My Life

My Family:

Joseph DeStasio Sr. & Miriam Lucille Baragone DeStasio, My Late Parents.

Andrea Jean DeStasio McIntosh, My Older Sister and Their Families.

Joseph DeStasio Jr., My Younger and Only Brother and Their Families.

Donna Marie DeStasio Wagner, My Younger Sister and Their Families.

My Children:

Eileen, Rebekah, Rachel, S. Michael,

Jennifer, Sharon, Tara, Stephanie,

Apryll, Mikaelah, & M. Trevor

and THEIR Families!!

ACKNOWLEDGEMENTS

First and foremost, I express, deeply, my sincere gratitude to our Heavenly Father for blessing me with the gift and talent of writing! I know I could not do what I do without His assistance.

I also want to acknowledge and express gratitude to the members of my birth family—Joseph Sr., Miriam, Andrea, Joseph Junior, and Donna. All the experiences of my childhood years, experiences that taught me so very much and enabled me to reveal my true self to myself, came about through my experiences and relationships with them.

And, of course, it goes without saying, but I will say it anyway: I also want to acknowledge and note my gratitude to my children, Eileen, Rebekah, Rachel, S. Michael, Jennifer, Sharon, Tara, Stephanie, Apryll, Mikaelah, and M. Trevor, and their families! Through multiple things they said to me, over multiple years, I finally came to the realization that

Heavenly Father gave me the gift of writing and opened the doors to these experiences because He knew that by sharing them with others, others could feel His love too.

And He definitely wants us all to know that He, Heavenly Father, Heavenly Mother, and Jehovah truly do loves us!!!

INTRODUCTION

There are sixteen books in this series, which I refer to as, *"The Ellie Series."* All of the characters in these stories portray real people from my life. The main characters depict the members of my family: Daddy is my daddy; Mommy is my mommy; Jeannie is my older sister; Junior is my brother; Maria is my younger sister, and Ellie is me. Now, those are not our actual first names, but they do reference us.

The first story in the series presents our Heavenly Father's Plan of Salvation and takes place in the Pre-Earth World. Now, of course, because we all—when we were born—received what is known as The Veil of Forgetfulness, I do not actually remember everything from or about the Pre-Earth World, but I do know about and understand it from much study and worship as a member of The Church of Jesus Christ of Latter-Day Saints, and memories restored to me through the Holy Spirit. So, from this story there is much truth to be learned.

The last story in the series is set in the Post-Mortal World, and presents a depiction of what happens to us after this life. Again, because I have not gone there yet, I cannot say I 'remember' this. But I have also learned about the Post-Mortal World from much study and worship as a member of The Church of Jesus Christ of Latter-Day Saints.

All of the other stories are based on true events from my life; events that actually occurred when and how they are depicted in these stories. I chose these events because they are among the many occurrences in my life that presented—or revealed that which I already knew without having to be taught—Principles of Eternal Truths.

Also, I chose these events as the settings for my stories because they depict wonderful learning moments from my childhood and adolescent years, lessons that have blessed and benefited me throughout the whole of my life and will forever continue to do so. Also, through these great truths and their consequences in my life, I have been able to share them with many others, whose lives have also been blessed by them.

So, please read and enjoy, then care and share the messages and stories with others!!

Now, there are also a couple of things you can look for:

In each story, the title of the previous story is presented in *italicized* form, the title of the next story is presented in *Capitalized Italicized* form, and the title of the story being read is presented in **emboldened** form.

Also, every story has at least one word that is uncommon or 'created.'

So, as you read, search, find, and have fun!

RIGHT FROM THE BEGINNING

For a little lady, new to the mortal world, it was remarkably amazing how much Ellie could fill life with adventure! She was quite talented and naturally good at a lot of things, most of which, were things that Daddy and Mommy definitely preferred she would not have been so good at!!

Now, you may be wondering, 'What were those things?' Well, just in case you are wondering and even if you are not, I will tell you what those things were, but only just a few of them. If I tried to tell you what all of them were, you would be sitting there listening to me for the next trazillion years! Okay, maybe not that long, but you definitely would be listening for a time longer than you would probably prefer to be listening. Now, moving on...

One of the things Ellie was really good at was movement! Yep! She was always in motion! When Daddy or Mommy held her, she would wiggle and wriggle until it was almost nigh to impossible for Daddy or Mommy to hold her. She could bounce and bump in her crib, on the floor, in anybody's lap. She even squirmed and squiggled when she was sleeping. Ellie simply could not stay still! Nope! Not still at all!! There was no such thing as a motionless moment for Ellie. Well, at least not until Mommy tried to put her to sleep. Then...

Ellie was the best possum player on this side of the universe! That was another one of her amazing talents! When she wanted to, and no one ever could determine what made her want to, she could lay as still as a cement porch step, no twitching, no kicking, no crying. (Now, that was an accomplishment! But we will get to that later.) Truth be told, when Ellie was playing possum, there was no indication at all that she was actually awake. Nope! None!! Why, she could make ANYONE believe she was asleep: Daddy, Mommy, big sister Jeannie, even Nonna.

Quick Side Note: Nonna was Daddy's Mom, so she was Ellie's grandmother. Nonna is the Italian way of saying Grandmother, and Italian is what Ellie's family is. Now, back to the other side.

No, wait! Before we go back to the other side, and so that you can understand just how good Ellie was at possum playing, listen to this story from her toddlerhood.

There was one time, when Ellie was about a year old, that Nonna was visiting the Stations—uh, that is the family's last name, Stations—and it was getting pretty late, late enough for Ellie to be going to bed. Of course, Nonna, being the loving, helpful person that she was, picked up Ellie, sat down on the sofa, and began patting her back as she sang some sweet baby-bed-time-songs. After a bit of a while, but not too big of a bit, Ellie 'fell asleep,' or so Nonna thought.

Mommy assured Nonna that Ellie was not asleep, but so certain was Nonna that Ellie was asleep that she took her upstairs, put her in her bed, and then went back downstairs. However, about the time that Nonna was settling down on the sofa again, Mommy said, "Nonna, look who is coming down the stairs."

Well, Nonna looked and who do you think she saw?

"Was it Ellie?" you are probably asking.

Well, if you are, you are right! Yes, Nonna saw Ellie scooting down the steps! Then with the biggest grin little Ellie could muster, she scampered across the living room to Nonna, reached her arms up, letting Nonna know that she wanted her to pick her up, which Nonna did, and then settled herself back down in Nonna's lap, and 'went back to sleep.' Or should I say, she went back to possum playing, which she did so well that one might wonder if she was even a living baby or just the best-ever life-size doll. Anyway, that time, Nonna decided to just hold little Ellie, until Daddy or Mommy decided it was time to take her up to her bed. Okay, now that you understand all of that—how well Ellie could play possum—we can go back to the other side.

When talking about how much she could move, we cannot forget to mention how well, Ellie could 'roll', especially, down the stairs! Yep! She set that record too! She could roll better and faster than Daddy's basketball, baseball, soccer ball, or even his globe! Now, you may be wondering, 'How did she accomplish this?' Well, I will tell you.

Although the step riser was higher than she was tall—okay, not really, we just needed a little drama setting here—anyway, she tried to crawl up the stairs any and every time she got the chance, which she took every time she was put down on the floor. Sometimes, she would make it to the third step; a few times, she got as far as the sixth step; once, she even made it to the ninth step!

Now, it was not the going up that was the problem; it was the coming down. Going up, she simply pulled with her hands and pushed with her feet, one step, then another, and anoth… okay, you have the idea. So anyway, she just kept climbing until someone, with a tone that sounded like an alarm, would say, "Ellie Stations, what are you doing?!"

That always made Ellie jump, which always made Ellie lose hold of the step, which always ended with Ellie rolling down the steps like a ball, hitting the wall when she landed on the landing. Did she cry? Mmmm, no, not right away. Apparently, Ellie thought it was fun; so, she laughed and laughed and laughed until she realized that she hurt. THEN, she cried and cried and cried until Mommy or Daddy picked her up, held her close, assured her she was okay, and sang to her until she became restless, and wiggled and wriggled wildly enough to be put down before she 'escaped the hold' and fell to the floor. But as soon as she was put down, she headed to the stairs to start the climb again. Of course, Daddy or Mommy intervened.

So, as I said before, other than when she was playing possum, one of the things that Ellie did not bring with her into this new world called Earth-Life, was the ability to stay still. Nope! Ellie was always moving—awake or asleep—still was not her skill!!

Okay, so now you should understand why Ellie's lack of the skill to stay still was quite the... uhm... should I call it an adventure for Daddy and Mommy? Yes! I should, because it definitely was one of the things that brought about a lot of the Station's adventures, but it was not the only one. No, definitely not the only one. Why, from the time Ellie was born, there were many different ways that she made life interesting.

For one, she set the record for crying, and then reset it, and reset it, and rese... well, you get the idea. Now, not only could she cry for a loooooonnng time, but she could cry over anything, everything, and nothing at all! And, when Ellie cried, her symphonic screams could be heard on the other side of the universe!

Oh, and no one could spit food as far as Ellie could! Carrots covered the highchair tray (and Mommy's dress). Green beans carpeted the floor (and Mommy's shoes). Meat plastered the wall across the room (and Daddy when he was walking by). Yep, everything that went into her mouth came right back out of her mouth. Well, almost everything. There was one thing she did not spit out—water—and it appeared that she could not get enough of that! No matter how much Mommy gave her, she always cried for more!

Yes, **Right from the Beginning**, Ellie was quite the master of accomplishment at many things, but the one thing Ellie could not do, was the one thing her mommy most wanted her to do—sleep; I mean really sleep, not just play possum! Mommy would sing to her every song she knew and even made up a few more. Mommy would walk around the room, around the house with her for longer than it took a Piper J-3 Cub to fly from the Airport in Reading, Pennsylvania, to the boardwalk by the Atlantic Ocean in Wildwood, New Jersey (well, okay, maybe not that long). Mommy would sit on the bottom step of the attic stairs, rocking, and rocking, and ro... well, you know what I mean, until Mommy was just about asleep! But Ellie?

Well, cuddled in Mommy's arms, she was quiet — most of the time; she was peaceful—oftentimes; she was even possum playing, sometimes; but she was not asleep, at least not until it was time for Daddy and Mommy to get up for the start of another day! Now, that could be good, if it was helping them get up *in time for church*, or work, or... but every day?!

Yes, Ellie began life with some challenges. Or should we say Ellie began life as a challenge? Either way, Ellie's first year, and every year after that, was an interesting one!

Now, about this first year, everybody knows, or maybe almost everybody probably knows, that no one is supposed to be able to remember anything from their first year of life, but Ellie did. That was another one of her amazing accomplishments. She never seemed to forget anything. She remembered everything she saw. She remembered everything she heard. She remembered everything she felt. She remembered everything she did. She even, as Daddy and Mommy quickly learned, remembered everything they wanted her to forget. Sometimes, it was apparent, even at the moment, that Ellie was not going to forget what she was learning. Other times, it was not apparent until sometime later, that Ellie had not forgotten… whatever it was she had not forgotten, and one of her first-year memories was just like that.

Of course, with this particular memory, Ellie did not know that she was remembering it when it happened. In fact, she was well past the age of infancy when she was informed by Mommy that what she had remembered had to have occurred before she was nine months old. Mommy was convinced of that because that was when—at nine months old—she no longer put Ellie in the crib.

Now, you may be wondering, 'Why did she take Ellie out of the crib at nine months old?' Well, I will tell you why. Ellie began climbing out of the crib when she was about six months old. Yes! You read that right, six-months-old!

Now, side note here, that abilityto climb out of the crib, even before she could walk, or even crawl very well, was a forewarning to Daddy and Mommy that Ellie would somehow, in some way, be able to do things that just could not be done and sometimes probably should not be done, either by someone as small as Ellie, or by anyone at all!! And of course, those would be the things that Ellie would be most interested in doing, like crib climbing!

At first, it was not the easiest endeavor that Ellie chose to challenge. She would wiggle her way through the bars on the side of the crib, and then fall gracelessly to the floor.

'Wait! What?! Wiggle THROUGH the bars? How was that possible?' you may be asking. Well, here is your answer. When Ellie was a baby, which was some time ago, cribs were made a bit differently than they are today. The bars were actually farther apart making the space between them a bit bigger, and Ellie, being as tiny as she was, had no problem fitting through them. The problem Ellie had was landing.

Naturally, she was too small to just step down to the floor, so she always ended up falling down to the floor, and that did not feel good. So, of course, she got more practice crying, not that she needed it. Now, because of that—the way the fall felt when Ellie 'climbed' out of the crib—after Mommy soothed her and put her back in the crib, she would stay there… well, at least for a bit of a while.

But it was not long before Ellie was able to teach herself how to climb through the bars and land on the floor with a little less force; she just kept hold of the bar and slid down until the floor touched her feet, and then she let go. Of course, Mommy would still put her back into the crib, but Ellie was only inclined to stay there for just a tab bit of a while.

However, by the time she was... oh... about eigh... maybe nine months old, there was no point in putting Ellie in the crib at all, not for nighttime sleep, not for daytime naps, not for any reason. Because as soon as she was put into the crib, or as soon as she woke up, if she was asleep when she was put into the crib and she would climb out of the crib; she simply would just not stay in the crib for any bit of a while!

Now, back to the track! What was that memory? This was that memory.

It was another typical bedtime war. Mommy sang to Ellie every song that had ever been written. (Well, not really every song, but it sure sounded like that!) Did Ellie go to sleep? Nope! Ellie just cried, louder than a full Philharmonic Orchestra! Maybe she thought she had to be Mommy's 'musician.'

Mommy walked all over the state of Pennsylvania with Ellie. (Uh, okay, so that is a bit of an exaggeration too, but it sure felt like that to Mommy!) Did Ellie go to sleep? Nope! Ellie just wiggled and wriggled, kicking her feet faster than Harrison Dillard ran in order to win the Gold Medal in the 1952 Olympics! (Well, okay, maybe not that fast, but fast enough to make it hard for Mommy to hold her. Soooo...)

Mommy sat down on the bottom attic step, cuddled Ellie in her arms while resting her on her lap, and swayed back and forth, and forth and back, and back and fo... you know the word; she swayed until she was as seasick as a beluga whale in a tidal wave. (Well, maybe not; belugas probably never get seasick.) Did Ellie go to sleep? Nope! But Ellie did fall into 'possum mode.'

Of course, Mommy knew that if she put Ellie down, Ellie would just 'wake up.' So, taking advantage of Ellie's relaxed state (which was not something often experienced by Ellie), Mommy took her back downstairs to the living room. She sat down in the corner of the couch, which was her favorite place to relax, propped Ellie up on her lap, and picked up a Fairly Tale Book from the end-table. She called for Jeannie, Ellie's older sister, who was just two years old at that time, and then, after Daddy got Jeannie settled on the couch next to her, Mommy began to read. As she did, both Jeannie and Ellie looked at the pictures in the book. Of course, as was always the case, Mommy had to read quite a few stories before anyone fell asleep.

Who fell asleep first? Was it Ellie? Nope! It was Jeannie!

Who fell asleep next? Was it Ellie? Nope! It was Daddy!

So, Mommy got up, walked around with Ellie, sang to her, and rocked her. All the while, Ellie was wiggling and wriggling, squirming and squiggling, until, after what felt like a never-ending drama to Mommy, she finally wandered off into dreamland.

Mommy took Ellie upstairs and put her in her crib in the bedroom at the top of the steps, left the door open, and went back down to the living room. She then took Jeannie, who was still asleep, upstairs and tucked her into her bed, which was in the same room as Ellie's crib. Then she returned to the living room to enjoy some sweetheart time with Daddy.

They sat down on the couch together to watch a little bit of late-night T.V. before it went off the air at midnight, but even before that, probably less than an hour later, they heard Ellie crying. Now, they might have felt a little frustrated if Ellie's cry sounded like it usually did, expressing the message, 'Hey! Get me out of here!' But this time, Ellie's cry sounded more like a plea for help. She sounded like she was frightened!

Naturally, Daddy and Mommy quickly arose from the couch, hustled across the living room, and bounded up the stairs, thinking that Ellie had probably tried to climb out of the crib again and fell to the floor. But that was not what they found when they entered the room.

Ellie was still in the crib, sitting up, holding onto the bars, and crying and shaking. Clearly, Ellie was frightened! But from what?! There was no one and nothing in the room that had not always been there or that should not be there. There were no shadows that could have scared her. There were not even any frightening sounds. So, what could it have been?

Obviously, Ellie could not tell them; she could not even talk yet, well, maybe a word here or something that sounded like a word there, but no sentences, no conversations. And there were no other hints either. Nope! Nothing! There really was just no way for them to know.

Anyway, Mommy picked up Ellie and began to soothe her with sweet, soft words and a comforting pat, pat, pat on the back, but Ellie just continued to cry. With the hope that Ellie's crying would not wake up Jeannie, Mommy took her to the other bedroom that was at the top of the stairs, which was their Daddy's and Mommy's bedroom, and sang sweet, quiet songs while walking all around the room. But that seemed to make no difference either; Ellie just kept crying. Seeing that Mommy was quite tired, after all, it was rather late. Daddy took Ellie in his arms and, while swaying back and forth, also tried to soothe her with soft humming and comforting back pats, but to no avail; she just could not stop crying. It was not until he picked up his Rosary from off the dresser, and swayed it from side to side, in front of her, that Ellie began to stop crying.

"Hmmm," Daddy whispered softly to Mommy, who had sat down on the bed in front of them, "that is interesting." Mommy got up to see what he was talking about and as Daddy continued to sway the Rosary in front of Ellie, Mommy could see what Daddy was seeing. As they both followed Ellie's gaze, they concluded that she was looking at the cross, which held the image of Jesus.

Daddy stopped swaying the Rosary, held the cross up in front of Ellie and, as both Daddy and Mommy watched her, they saw her expression change from what they identified as a bit of curious calm to a beaming smile of peace. It seemed that Ellie, who they thought was too young to know God, was recognizing Jesus.

"I think we have a little spiritual one here," Daddy said to Mommy, who nodded her head in agreement. It was not too long after that that Ellie finally wandered back into dreamland.

After giving Ellie one more loving, 'Daddy-Hug' and a kiss on the cheek, he handed Ellie to Mommy, who gave her one more loving 'Mommy-Hug' and a kiss on the other cheek. After wrapping Ellie's blanket around her, Mommy took her back to her bedroom and gently laid her down in her crib, where she finally slept through the night—well, at least most of it.

But what was it that scared Ellie that night? Daddy did not know. Mommy did not know. Jeannie had not even been awake, so, of course, she did not know. And Ellie could not tell them. However, a couple of years later, when Ellie was two years old, while Mommy was reading the story *"Jack and the Beanstalk"* to Ellie and Jeannie, that question was answered, and this was that answer.

It was just another, same as always, snuggly bedtime storytime. Daddy was sitting across the room in his comfy oversized chair, reading the newspaper. Mommy was sitting in the corner seat of the couch, where she always liked to sit, and Ellie, who was holding her favorite stuffed animal—a horse—was snuggled between Mommy and Jeannie. Mommy had already read several stories, but Ellie and Jeannie were still wide awake, so Mommy started reading another story. Well, it was not long before Ellie began to get a little restless. The more Mommy read; the more restless Ellie became.

Now, you might think her restlessness would get some attention. But it really did not. I mean, why would it? Remember, Ellie never sat still. Ellie never stood still. Ellie never laid still. Ellie did not seem to know what it meant to be still. So, her restlessness did not seem to be any more than usual, until…

Suddenly, when Mommy was about half-way through the story, Ellie quickly jumped off the couch, hustled across the room, and bounded up the stairs, as fast as a two-years-old could bound, to Daddy's and Mommy's room, where she found Daddy's Rosary on his dresser. With his Rosary held tightly in her hand, she scurried back down the stairs—well, her scurry was more like a bounce—she 'danced' across the room, actually, she hopped, and then she tried to climb back up onto the sofa, with all the grace of a falling acorn. Finally, with Jeannie's help, Ellie was back up on the couch, holding her stuffed horse, and cuddled between Mommy and Jeannie.

Noticing that Ellie had something in her hand, Mommy asked, "Ellie, what do you have?"

"This," Ellie answered matter-of-factly, but with a touch of shyness too, while holding up the Rosary so Mommy could see it.

"What are you doing with that?" Mommy asked, quizzically.

Listening to the exchange between Mommy and Ellie, and noticing that it was his Rosary that Ellie was holding, Daddy put down the newspaper, walked over to the couch and squatted down in front of Ellie, as she quietly replied, "It makes me feel good."

Daddy watched Ellie, as Ellie continued to look at the image of Jesus. Mommy watched Ellie too. In fact, so did Jeannie, but no one said anything until...

Remembering that it was the Rosary that seemed to calm Ellie the night that they, Daddy and Mommy, found her crying with fright in her crib, Daddy asked, "Are you afraid of something?"

Ellie looked down at the Rosary. Then, as she wrapped it around her hands, and with a few tears in her eyes while rocking back and forth, she answered softly and slowly but sweetly, "Jackie scares me!"

"What?" Mommy asked curiously and with concern, "Why?"

Ellie continued to restlessly rock back and forth. She even began to shake a little bit, enough for Jeannie, who, even though she was only four- years old, could see that Ellie, whom she very much loved, was sort of... kind of... a little bit scared. So, she held onto Ellie's arm, snuggling a little bit closer, as Ellie began to explain, "His stalk came up the steps one time. It was really big! And really fat!! And... and... it came across the floor and... and came in my room."

Daddy moved closer to Ellie and put his hand on her knee for comfort, as she continued, "It... it... it came to my bed, and..."

Ellie, who was now shaking quite a bit, looked up at Daddy, then at Mommy, then at Jeannie, then back to Daddy, who wiped away her tears, and then back down at the Rosary, as she finished explaining, "Jackie's stalk stood up and... and it was going to get me!" Then, with a hint of a smile, she looked up at Mommy and said, "But you and Daddy came up the steps and saved me!" Then, looking again at the Rosary, she sweetly added, "And Jesus made me feel better! I love Him!"

Mommy and Daddy immediately understood! Ellie, at such a young age, had had a bad dream, and it was inspired by the story of "Jack and the Beanstalk" that Mommy had been reading to them before bed that night. Ellie was too young, at that time, to understand that the story was not real. She was too young to put words to her feelings, but she could imagine the images she had seen in the book, and that was what created, perhaps the first, but definitely and sadly, not the only nightmare that Ellie ever had. It seemed to Daddy and Mommy that Ellie had an amazing ability to imagine and create. And that was good, in most ways, most of the time, but not when it was nightmares that were being created.

In that nightmare, when Ellie was only about eight or nine months old, the big, green, giant beanstalk had slithered up the stairs, probably the same way it had grown up beyond the clouds, in the story. It had slithered across the top step, into the bedroom and across the floor to the crib, probably the way it had moved across the land of the Giant. Then, it stretched up, above and over the side of the crib.

Ellie, being just a baby, could not have known that what she was seeing was only a dream. So, it was that dream that had frightened her awake! As she sat in the crib, holding onto the sidebar, though the stalk was gone, so real had the nightmare been to her, that she continued crying even when she could see that there was no stalk to see. It was not until Daddy and Mommy came upstairs and took care of her, and Jesus comforted her, that she was able to calm down and go back to sleep.

Daddy picked Ellie up off the couch, hugged her tightly and then comforted her by taking the time to explain that the story was just make-believe. Jackie was not a real boy and, while there are some very tall people, there are no real giants, at least not like the one in that story, anywhere. Bean stalks most certainly never grow that tall; even if they did, being stuck in the ground, they cannot slither anywhere. And nobody lives in the clouds.

After Ellie relaxed and was again calm, Daddy put her back down on the couch between Mommy and Jeannie, where she picked up her stuffed horse, gave it a great big, little hug, while whispering, *My Horsey, My Horsey, My Horsey,* and then he sat down on the other side of Jeannie. Before beginning to read a different Fairy Tale, Mommy cuddled Ellie beside her. She watched Ellie wrap and rewrap and rewrap the Rosary around her hands. Daddy was watching Ellie too.

Then, in the same instant, Daddy and Mommy looked over at each other. It was quite apparent that they both were realizing that while they had been the ones to comfort Ellie, the night of her nightmare, with songs, hugs, pats, and hums, it was really Jesus who had made it possible for Ellie to feel good, in the face of something bad. They both were very pleased to know that Ellie, **Right from the Beginning,** knew that she could turn to Jesus for comfort.

ABOUT THE AUTHOR

Eileen DiStasio-Clark is the second oldest of four children. She is the mother of eleven children and grandmother to twenty-three grandchildren, to date. As a member of The Church of Jesus Christ of Latter-Day Saints, she serves in various positions, teaching, leading, and ministering to children, youth, and adults. Currently, she is also a Family History Missionary. Eileen established the Pursuit of Excellence Institute of Family Education, a non-profit organization focused on strengthening the family. Presently she holds an A.A., a B.A., and an M.A. in Clinical Psychology and is working on the completion of her Doctoral Degree.

www.ingramcontent.com/pod-product-compliance
Lightning Source LLC
Chambersburg PA
CBHW041235060526
44107CB00136BA/737